THE 4 FUNDAMENTALS OF
FAMILY
PROSPERITY

HOW WEALTHY FAMILIES
PROTECT THEIR WEALTH AND AVOID
GENERATIONAL FINANCIAL FAILURE

NICHOLAS CHARLES FCCA

WRITING MATTERS PUBLISHING

The Four Fundamentals of Family Prosperity:
How wealthy families protect their wealth and avoid generational financial failure

First published in October 2018

Writing Matters Publishing (UK)
info@writingmatterspublishing.com
www.writingmatterspublishing.com

ISBN 978-1-912774-10-4 (Kindle)
ISBN 978-1-912774-11-1 (Pbk)

Nicholas Charles

DEDICATION

To my wife Andrea and my two amazing children, Christina and Leonidas. You truly inspire me in my life to be the best I can be.

Contents

The Four Fundamentals
Of Family Prosperity At A Glance

Long-term studies show that 90% of wealthy families fail financially within three generations, and there is a 70% likelihood that a family will lose all their wealth within just two generations.

Imagine spending all your life working in order to build a business and accumulate wealth that should, by right, establish your legacy and family name. Yet, by the time your grandchildren come of age, the wealth that you worked so hard to establish has completely GONE!

This book uncovers the stories and the data that supports these alarming facts and explains what you and your family need to do to avoid becoming yet another sad statistic. You will be surprised to discover what is really required to both retain and grow your family's wealth.

The solution to multi-generational financial success is a holistic one that's rarely considered by your traditional professional advisors

The question that needs to be answered is, "Do you want to be like 90% of people who simply leave their assets in a will or do you want to start building an inspirational legacy that will last beyond the lives of your children and grandchildren?"

This book reveals the research which proves that only a family with a purpose greater than its individual needs has the foundations required to experience multi-generational wealth.

Families need to appreciate the business of being a family. This book will explain what is required to successfully achieve multi-generational wealth and, even more importantly, a happy family.

Shirtsleeves to shirtsleeves in three generations is not just a saying. When my father was just a boy, he experienced the total loss of an entire family fortune. After rebuilding our wealth from scratch, I was determined to find out how we could break this inevitable cycle.

As a qualified accountant and tax advisor, I have saved my clients millions of pounds only to question what the point of it is when they end up losing their wealth anyway. Family breakdown will always lead to financial meltdown.

The most crucial areas that are often overlooked by traditional professional advisors include structured effective communication, understanding family values, having a purposeful family vision, preparing the heirs, wealth education and appreciation, sustainable philanthropy and aligned accountable professional advisors. These areas are simply not dealt with by 'traditional' professional services. These aspects are crucial for your family's wealth legacy and must be in place if you wish to establish family governance that will last for multiple generations to come.

Every aspect of multi-generational wealth is incorporated in the four fundamental components, which are:

• Effective Communication

• Wealth education and preparing the heirs

• Sustainable philanthropy

• Aligned professional advisors who are accountable to the family's vision

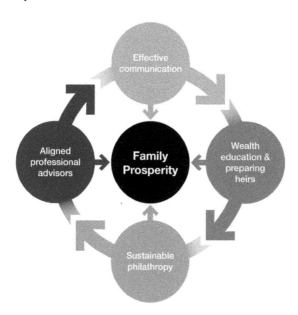

If any of these four components is not put fully in place, your family will be doomed to be among the 90% that fail financially.

Your family's prosperity includes not only financial wealth, but also human and intellectual capital, so it is important that your family works together to pass this down from generation to generation.

It is essential to appreciate that the application of these four components will transform the future prosperity of your family in the short, medium and long term.

Preface:
The Pains Of The Second Generation Of Wealthy Families (And Why Nobody Understands Them)

This is a story about a young man who came from a wonderful family, had a great upbringing, described his position as second generation wealth yet felt very lost and alone in his twenties. His life was direction-less and seemingly going nowhere although on the face of it he had everything, deep down he felt trapped and frustrated because not only could he not describe his emotions, but he felt stupid to even ask for help. How could this be? There was no immediate tragedy, he was a healthy young man, he came from a good family, money had never been an issue and having qualified as an accountant he even had an element of academic and professional success. So, what the hell was the problem? Confused, alone, in darkness and unsure about the direction of his life this is not only my story, but what I have discovered to be a story that resonates with many other second-generation children of wealthy families.

I always wanted to achieve something great in my life. Initially I felt my purpose was to go to university, get a good qualification and then pass my professional accountancy exams first time. Although this stage of my life was difficult (university was both boring and the exams were tough) – I had a target, a goal and this drove me to achieve what I felt at the time was success. The problems began when I *reached* my goals, I simply did not know what to do with myself. I simply *fell* into the first job I found and at a blink of an eye three years passed in my life.

I fell into a zone that is so dangerous that it makes you feel stale and lethargic as it drains all the energy in your life – the comfort zone! I ended up working in my father's business something which I never wanted to do. I was frustrated and angry.

I didn't know my life purpose or vision. I felt burdened with the expectations of carrying on my father's legacy and to continue looking after the family which included my two siblings. I had nowhere to go and I felt that nobody understood my position. I was deeply frustrated, I couldn't describe what was eating me inside, and I hid my true emotions from the rest of the world. I blamed my father for the position I found myself in my life and hid behind this blame.

You see my father came to this country in his early twenties with just the clothes on his back. This gave him the drive and ambition to become the self-made success he is today. He worked hard to be able to provide for his children the life he never had, and he succeeded.

When I was growing up I experienced my father's success evolving. From the outside looking in I had an easy life. However, being given an easy life creates different problems as I would soon realise growing up.

What was immediately apparent to me was an in-built fear of loss and failure that has remained with me until today. My Great Grandfather (my father's grandfather) was in his day very successful and wealthy.

He was a tall powerfully built man who had a very savvy business mind. Based in Cyprus, those that controlled the land controlled the wealth (which is not too dissimilar to today). My Great Grandfather controlled virtually all the land and the produce it created in his Cypriot village of Dikomo (today called Dikmen in the occupied area of Cyprus).

His son (my grandfather) inherited a great fortune and had a very privileged childhood. Unfortunately, he didn't have the stomach for business - in fact he didn't want to learn about finances. He gave away most of the land he inherited to his eldest children without thought or care and what remained he squandered. By the time my father (who was the second youngest of eight children) was seven the wealth had gone.

My father became self-made successful entrepreneur so in my mind I had the burden of thinking that historically, in accordance to our family cycle I was due to lose it all.

I was to later discover that this process had a name: *shirtsleeves to shirtsleeves in three generations.*

My worries of this were compounded when I discovered extensive research on *generational family wealth* which confirmed that 70% of wealthy families lose their wealth within two generations and over 90% lose it all within three generations!

I followed my father's footsteps but always wanted to create something for myself. I had no love for my existing work and felt trapped in a cycle that was leading me nowhere.

I was desperately searching for a *solution* even though I didn't know what the solution was. I bottled all my emotions and didn't appreciate that all my problems were simply an illusion that I had created myself. My life would only improve if I empowered myself to discover that the solution always rested within me.

Being lost gave me a reason to look for something better. I trained myself to become an expert in my field, to experiment and make the necessary mistakes which has made me the person I am today. As someone who would call himself second generation wealth, I had to discover something which comes very naturally to self-made millionaires (first generation wealth) and that is ambition!

Rather than fight my situation I embraced it. I had the choice to either moan or complain about my circumstances or to take control of my life. I looked at both the advantages and the disadvantages of who I was, where I was and my personal upbringing and loved them both equally.

My background gave me the insight knowledge of the struggles and pressures of second generation wealth and the potential stresses it can place on a family. As a professional I also realised there was a massive gap in the market for collective professional services that not only understood family dynamics and how it can impact the family wealth legacy but that also empathized with families.

The fact is all families contain persons with different value systems.

I have created a business that understands this and provides bespoke solutions that meets our clients (families) specific needs. By helping our clients communicate and understand each other's value systems they become empowered to keep and expand their wealth for generations. Vitally we also ensure that the existing advisors are aligned to work together to achieve the family's vision. This forms part of our strategy to help *bridge the gap* between families and their advisors.

I embraced my advantageous position which I thought was holding me back in my life. I learned about property investing and grew the family portfolio four-fold.

I have now built a team that has enabled my company *Charles Group* to become the hub for successful high net worth individuals and families. I am now using my experience and expertise to help facilitate the business of being a family. We help our clients to establish the four fundamental components of family prosperity.

I know how lonely and trapped it feels to be second generation wealth and the potentially destructive effect it can have on the family dynamic and legacy - your family does not have to be in the same position.

The Most Important Conversation Wealthy Families Need To Have

Imagine

You spend all your life working to build a business and accumulate the wealth that, by right, should establish your legacy and family name. Yet, by the time your grandchildren have come of age, the wealth that you worked so hard to establish has completely gone.

What I have just described is a scenario that plays itself out over and over again.

The most extensive study that has been conducted on this subject, by Roy Williams and Vic Preisser, involved 3,250 families over a 25 year period and proved that 90% of families will go from *shirtsleeves to shirtsleeves within three generations*. The 2014 *Forbes* billionaire family list further highlighted this fact by revealing that, of the 483 billionaire families analysed, less than 10 per cent were third generation!

This damning statistic even applies to families who we think have created far too much money for it to dissipate.

Look no further than the Vanderbilt family as a case study. In just 70 years, they went from $100 billion (in today's money) to declaring the first bankruptcy within the family. When the Vanderbilt family held a reunion in 1973, there was not a single millionaire among them.

"It has left me with nothing to hope for, with nothing definite to seek or strive for. Inherited wealth is a real handicap to happiness. It is a certain death to ambition as cocaine is to morality"

William K Vanderbilt *grandson of the self-made*
Cornelius Vanderbilt

Maybe you think that the Vanderbilt family was a one-off and no other family with such wealth could make similar mistakes? Some quick research, however, will prove you wrong.

The Hartfords

George Huntington Hartford II inherited $500 million in 1969 ($4.5 billion in today's money) from his famous grandfather of the same name. Unfortunately, through bad investments, the wealth disappeared and the grocery store business that his grandfather had established filed for bankruptcy in 2015.

The Strohs

In 1850, Bernard Stroh, a German immigrant, started and successfully built a brewery business in the United States, which was continued by his family heirs. At its peak in the 1980s, the Stroh brand became one of the fastest growing companies in America and the country's third largest brewing company.

According to *Forbes*, the family at the time was worth $700 million. Just by matching the S&P 500, the family would be currently worth $9 billion. Today, the Strohs have ceased to exist as a family business or collective entity.

Although it took them a little longer than the average, it appears that the Stroh family has gone from *shirtsleeves to shirtsleeves* in six generations.

> "Hard as it is to build a family business designed to last in perpetuity, it's shockingly easy for any successor to tank it."
> **Kerry Dolan,** *Forbes Magazine*

Yes, these families had the best estate and financial planning in place. We assume that they continued to review their estate planning with their professional advisors regularly and kept it up to date. So why did these families fail to retain their wealth for multiple generations?

The main reasons why families fail financially continues to surprise many professionals, such as accountants and financial advisors, as poor tax and estate planning is not the main cause. In fact, the most important issues that undermine the successful transfer of family wealth is poor communication and a lack of trust.

Other causes of family financial failure (or post-transition failure) are having heirs who are unprepared for their future roles and responsibilities and the lack of a mission that has been agreed upon by the family.

To highlight how few families, retain their wealth over multiple generations, we only need to review and compare the 2014 *Forbes* billionaire list with the *Forbes* richest family list.

Of the 483 billionaires analysed, 321 — about two thirds — were first generation and only 20 per cent second generation. Less than 10 per cent were third generation.

Why Is This A Conversation Worth Having, Now?

The research is very clear: 70% of families will lose all their wealth within just two generations and more than 90% will lose it within three generations.

Typically, the first generation *makes* it; the second generation, if successful, *sustains* it; and the third generation *spends or loses* it. Statistically your family will very likely experience shirt sleeves to shirtsleeves in just three generations.

In our experience, most of our enquiries about preserving and growing family wealth come from the second generation; typically, the eldest male sibling.

In most cases, they are inheriting their parent's legacy. Sadly, in most cases, the first generation are reluctant to hand over the financial reigns and usually pass before they establish the controls and systems discussed in this book.

The second generation really do want to protect and grow the asset base. Justifiably they have concerns about who they can turn to for support and clear advice regarding their obligations to their parents, and siblings and extended family. Like their parents, they also have concerns about the next generation.

Our typical client is in their mid-40s plus and they manage a £25 million plus family wealth base of property, shares, cash and businesses.

Invariably, they feel worried about who they can trust.

Often, they want advice but don't know what advice they are seeking.

When they eventually do seek advice, they ask about taxes, inheritance tax and financial planning. They ask about investing and growth. They express concerns about existing complex and often convoluted or outdated, high risk investment structures.

However, these are not the main reasons why families fail financially.

Usually, they are concerned that they will appear naive or inexperienced. Importantly, their primary concern is about keeping family wealth intact, but they don't want to appear unwise.

They will express concerns about the next generation and are usually surprised that such a thing as preparing heirs, exists.

And, most are only starting to realise that the real job is keeping the family intact.

What Really Counts?

Whilst many professionals have an opinion on how to protect family wealth long term, the reality is that very few really understand and appreciate the fundamental issues. Even fewer know what the solutions are to sustain and grow family wealth for multiple generations.

In our experience as specialists in successfully dealing with wealthy family clients, as tax accountants and more importantly as a family with a family wealth dilemma; we have identified four things that absolutely must happen if you want to keep family wealth.

And, importantly, an intact and happy family.

You need to implement the *Four Fundamentals of Family Prosperity* and all four must be guided by a clear family vision and purpose:

1. Effective communication between ALL family members

2. Wealth education and preparing the heirs

3. Sustainable philanthropy

4. Aligned professional advisors

When all four are in place, your family will have secured, what we call at the *Charles Group*, the *Pyramid of Prosperity™*.

Unfortunately, what we see instead of a clear vision is a disturbing lack of direction, confusion and an ad hoc approach to wealth and succession planning. Rather than having regular effective communication amongst family members we see silos, agendas, secrets, distrust, misunderstandings, arguments and sadly, excessive and costly litigation.

Instead of prepared heirs and clear family governance; the norm is the unexpected transfers of financial responsibility to heirs that are unprepared. Too often we see mismanagement and a disappointing trail of avoidable mistakes, expensive errors and oversights that with proper planning are easily avoidable.

If just one of the *Four Fundamentals* are not in place, then your family is at risk of generational family financial failure. This just not just mean bankruptcy but also chaos, a divided family and emotional devastation.

A family is like a vase and needs to be protected as such. Just like a vase once is breaks is does not matter how much effort you place is trying to fix it the cracks will always remain, and it will never look the same again. When a family argument escalates to a legal battle it's the same as throwing the vase on a stone floor – the damage is irreparable.

Wealth was created to make the family lives better and easier. It was never intended to distress, divide or destroy families. Yet history has shown that is exactly what happens to the majority of families which is why less than 10% of families successful retain and grow their wealth for more than three generations.

> "Anybody who thinks money will make you happy, hasn't got money."
> **David Geffen** – *Founder of DreamWorks*

Moving Forward Intentionally

As you read on you will hear the same advice repeatedly. The key to preserving and growing family wealth across generations is effective communication.

By effective we mean structured.

Over many years, we developed a method that helps a wealthy family to talk openly about family wealth.

That includes family days, setting up a family board and holding structured meetings, and professional reviews. It is essential for all the family members to understand where the family is today and what is its ideal destination (i.e. Vision for the future). The first step to securing the family's ideal future is to create effective, consistent communication.

It also sounds too formal, but if the goal is to preserve, protect and grow family wealth then these steps are required. They are not discretionary.

This book is designed to get you thinking and to perhaps start a needed conversation. To get you talking. We will cover several key principles - fundamentals

- that underpin what we know works about family wealth.

Again, the principle that underpins everything is effective communication. You will preserve and grow family wealth to the degree that you invest in embracing the types of effective communication we will discuss.

If your goal is to be a good steward of family wealth and develop knowledge and skills in this sensitive area, then this is a perfect place to start.

To that end, we want to empower families to overcome any internal and external factors that inhibit effective communication; and therefore, anything that will predictably prevent your family wealth from protecting and growing wealth for generations to come.

People with family wealth rarely need to be convinced. If you do, then that probably is the best reason to read this book carefully.

This book explores some of the key principles that need to be embraced in order to avoid financial catastrophe, regardless of whether you are worth £10 million or £10 billion.

Stages Of Family Wealth

Fact: 90% of families fail to retain their wealth for three generations.

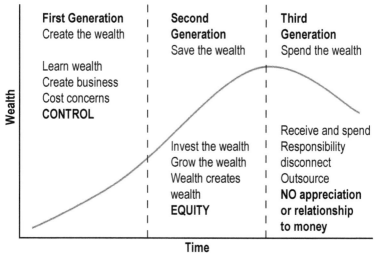

Stages of Family Wealth

The reason why financial failure in families is so common is mainly because the underlying problems are ignored. These issues will not magically go away. Nor can they be dealt with simply by financial or tax planning. Our message is simple: *Ignore this at your family's peril. Don't bury your head in the sand!*

"It requires a great deal of boldness and a great deal of caution
to make a great fortune; and when you have got it,
it requires ten times more wit to keep it."
Nathan Rothschild

Families are vulnerable and are unaware of the risks they face most of the time. It is clear that by possessing wealth, they will inevitably become a target. Do your children's current behaviours and activities demonstrate that they place a higher value on growing or spending wealth?

By looking back and studying how the world's richest families lost all their wealth, we have uncovered a similar pattern.

Sharks

No, I'm not talking about the ones that swim in the sea! I mean the fraudsters that will inevitably try to take your money.

How financially savvy are your family members to ensure this does not happen? Ponzi schemes, such as the one run by Bernard Madoff, cost investors approximately $18 billion. How confident are you today that your family will not be another victim of a similar scam?

Professional Advisors That Do Not Provide Value

Expensive does not mean good! If your advisors are not adding value to you, your family and your assets, then they should be treated as an unnecessary overhead and removed immediately!

Litigation

These are usually driven by emotional conflicts caused by a lack of transparency in financial dealings or simply a lack of good quality communication between family members. In fact, research has shown that poor communication and a lack of trust are the main reasons for loss of wealth over three generations. Why wait until you have passed away to explain (via your will) how and why you have decided to divide the financial assets between your chosen beneficiaries? Surely, such a sensitive and important topic needs to be discussed during your lifetime? Why risk your legacy being attacked by irate family members and the wealth, which you have worked so hard to create, becoming decimated by expensive legal bills?

To this day, the Rothschild family hold annual gatherings of all their family members, something they have been doing for over 200 years, and they affirm their family values that have sustained the family for generations at these events. Their vision for the future is sharpened and clarified at these annual events and if any family member does not attend, they are locked out of the family bank!

Negative Publicity In The Media And/or On The Internet

Any publicity that reveals how much wealth and assets you own can potentially cause a security issue.

A good example of this was the kidnapping of the grandson of John Paul Getty. Getty was the richest man in the world in 1966 and his grandson was eventually ransomed for $3.2 million in 1973; the maximum amount that was tax deductible at the time.

Poor Investment Decisions And/or Over-Leveraging

Money may attract money and although debt can be easy to raise to finance expensive acquisitions when everything is going well, any slight downturn in the economy, such as interest rate rises or a recession, may cause the debt to become unsustainable.

Just look at what happened in the 2008 recession: *Lehman Brothers*, the fourth largest investment bank in the USA, went bankrupt while *AIG*, *HBOS* and *Merrill Lynch* all came within a whisker of doing so and had to be bailed out by the government!

It all goes to prove that nobody, and certainly no family, is too big to fail.

Divorce

Nobody thinks about divorce when they get married, and yet approximately 42% of all marriages in the UK and the USA end in divorce, so the risks are factually high.

Whilst some divorces can be amicable, most are emotionally charged and, of course, result in expensive settlements and hefty legal fees.

Although there are ways to protect yourself from losing a large stake in your financial capital, the list below of some of the most famous divorces suggests that not everybody is utilising the correct advice:

- Craig and Wendy McCaw - More than $460 million
- Adnan and Soraya Khashoggi - $874 million (although numbers vary according to sources)
- Rupert and Anna Murdoch - $1.7 billion

The point is clear: factors that will undermine and devastate family wealth are both known and highly predictable.

However, many families still fail to understand the fundamental issues regarding preserving family wealth. Basically, this means that the biggest problem is the actual failure to understand the problem itself.

Before one can seek a solution, it is vital to understand the current risks the family currently faces and to get clear on where the family wants to be (i.e. a collective vision of the ideal future).

Unfortunately, despite the research and statistics that clearly shows most families will fail to retain their wealth for multiple generations, we still encounter families who feel that they are immune to this issues, because they feel everything is fine today, and it will always be so.

The Key Myths
Surrounding Family Wealth

"It takes a great deal of boldness and determination to create a vast fortune and ten times more wit to keep it!"
Nathan Rothschild

Wealth is surrounded by myths - the greatest one being: *there are no problems once you are financially independent.* Finances will never be the only problem we face in life, only those who do not have wealth consider obtaining it to be their biggest problem.

Having worked with many wealthy clients it became apparent to me that gaining a vast fortune was only the beginning. The problems that came with wealth, especially within the family dynamic were often ignored or simply treated as a problem for *tomorrow.*

Below, we have seven common *myths* because that is exactly what they are – *lies* that families keep telling themselves because they do not want to deal with or face the real problems that inevitably lie ahead.

Wealth brings with it an element of arrogance and feelings of invulnerability.

Great wealth provides power and options to do what one wishes. However, *shirtsleeves to shirtsleeves in three generations* is not simply a fairy story but a fact that affects over 90% of all wealthy families.

This list is not exhaustive but it does cover most of the myths I have faced both in my research and when dealing with families directly.

1. I/We Are Too Big Or Rich To Fail

The amount of money is irrelevant when it comes to protecting family wealth for multiple generations. Being too big to fail, stems from large blue-chip corporations who make the devastating mistake of getting comfortable with their size and, as such, fail to foresee problems.

Bankruptcies of conglomerates such as *Enron, WorldCom* and *Lehman Brothers* should provide ample warning that there is no such thing as being too big to fail.

The *2014 Forbes Family Rich List* contained less than 10% of families that were third generation wealth providing further evidence of the saying *shirtsleeves to shirtsleeves within three generations*.

Over the last 90 years there have been multiple cases of billionaire families reporting that they have lost all their wealth. The most famous example being the Vanderbilt family who lost today's equivalent of $100 billion within 75 years.

2. My Will is Perfectly Robust
So My Family Is Well-Protected

Although a Will is a highly valuable document it will not on its own protect your family wealth legacy. In fact, many Wills can be amended by family members after the donor has died!

The greatest mistake you can make is to avoid discussing the terms of your will during your lifetime with your family. It is *during* your life not *after* your death, where you need to put in place what is required to protect your family's wealth legacy. This should include regular conversations with your family about the assets, business and investments held by the family and to empower the relevant family members to manage these assets after you have passed.

Do not leave anything to chance and certainly do not allow your will to be the only time you discuss your assets with your family!

3. My Children Are Best Placed
To Take Over the Family Business

Most families will have a business or even a series of businesses and investments that they grow or maintain. Succession planning for the family business should take time, be properly planned and provided to the most qualified person.

Simply having the right surname should not be a sufficient reason to be given control over the family business.

Just like all companies if the wrong CEO is placed in charge it could lead to a financial disaster and even bankruptcy for that company. Family businesses are no different. Start by asking your family members if they are even interested in taking control of the family business! This should never be assumed.

Even if the family member has worked for a long period of time within the business, they may not want the responsibility, nor have the expertise to take control. Simply working for 20 years in a company does not necessarily mean that one is best qualified to be its CEO.

4. I Already Have Tax Advisors and Financial Advisors - My Family Is Perfectly Protected

We recommend that you build a team of professional advisors that can be trusted to serve the family's purpose and vision, on their own this team is not enough.

The Williams Group studied 3,250 families over a 25-year period to ascertain the causes of multi-generational financial failure. The results were truly staggering:

- 60% was caused by poor communication and lack of trust amongst family members

- 25% was because the heirs had not been properly prepared to receive the wealth

- 10% was because the family lacked a collective vision

- Only 5% was because of 'other' reasons

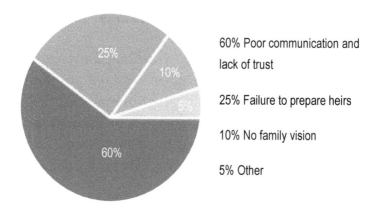

Despite the results from this research families still make the fundamental error of only focusing on the 5%! Traditional professional advice is not enough to help your family avoid losing all its wealth.

No advisor will ever be incentivised to look after the family wealth better than the family itself. Even the most trust worthy advisors need be given clear instructions and be made accountable via regular communication. We never expect any of our clients to become experts in tax or financial planning, but it would make sense to empower oneself to understand the advice and ask the right questions to the advisors. Simply giving money to an advisor and *hoping* they look after it will only lead to problems.

5. This Issue Will Resolve Itself

Thinking that everything will magically resolve by itself is probably the biggest mistake any family can make. Achieving multi-generational wealth is a process that requires effort and buy-in from *all family members*. The ideal scenario is to create a formal family governance structure; this is pro-active not passive.

Can your family afford to risk its financial future on hope?

- 70% of families will lose all their wealth within two generations

- Over 90% of families will lose it all within just three generations.

The statistics show that your family is already fighting an uphill battle. Hoping for the best is not a recommended strategy.

6. My Family Will Work It Out After I Have Gone

It is essential for all family members to be given formal roles within the family. Achieving multi-generational wealth successfully demands that the family needs to consider itself a business. Your success will be determined by the processes and structures you put in place.

We all appreciate that successful businesses have a Board of Directors. This Board meets regularly to discuss the vision of the business, what it has achieved since the previous meeting and what needs to be done to continue its drive towards success. Each director will have a specific role such as CEO, financial director, marketing director and COO. Wealthy families should be no different.

It is vital for wealthy families to have effective structures in place and to assign specific roles and responsibilities to each family member.

The works that needs to be done now during your lifetime and not left to chance. Formal structures and meetings in place will encourage open and honest communication amongst your whole family. Effective communication is essential for your family to achieve multi-generational wealth.

7. If It Is Not Broken ...

Finally, this really encapsulates all the above six points. Even if it is not openly stated, it is often inferred by the resistance to positive change. Things appear to be going well, so why do we need to engage in a family prosperity programme?

Simply, because the statistics are against you.

Essentially, you are relying on being the exceptional case - the exception to the rule. In our experience, very few families are!

You are at a decision point and you have a choice.

You can ignore a compelling body of research that shows that over 90% of all families will see their wealth evaporate by the third generation.

Or you can keep reading and discover how prudent families protect, retain and grow family wealth for multiple generations.

PART 1: THE SEVEN PRINCIPLES OF PROTECTING FAMILY WEALTH

What Can You Do To Retain Your Family Wealth?

We know that 70% of families will lose all their wealth within just two generations whilst over 90% will lose it within three generations. The question you should be asking yourself is: *how do I ensure that my family falls within the 10% category who retain their wealth legacy over multiple generations?*

How can you learn not just from the failings of the Vanderbilts, but also from the successes of well-known families, such as the Rockefellers?

Quite simply, families are able to retain and grow their wealth for multiple generations through planning that takes into account human capital, intellectual capital and financial capital.

First, however, let's discuss the seven key principles that you need to inspect and consider in order to assess whether your family will grow or blow your family wealth.

Before we explain these four fundamentals, let's first however, discuss the seven key areas that you need to consider in order to assess whether your family will *grow* or *blow* your family's wealth.

They are:

- Values, Goals and Ambitions
- Establishing a Family Vision
- Aligning Your Professional Power Team to The Family Vision
- Making Sure That The Next Generation Feel At Ease With Their Professional Power Team
- Effective Communication
- Getting the Next Generation To Understand And Appreciate Wealth
- Getting a Mentor and Trustee For Both the Family and The Next Generation

And there are four fundamental components that ensure family prosperity. They are:

- Effective Communication
- Wealth Education and Preparing the Heirs
- Sustainable Philanthropy
- Aligned and Accountable Professional Advisors

Let's look at the seven key areas in more detail.

1. Values, Goals and Ambitions

Understanding and appreciating
the different values of each member of the family

The person planning their estate is often first generation. He/she may think differently about money and will certainly have different views about work. After all, they will have come from nothing before creating a wealthy platform/foundation for the family through hard work and endeavour.

Your children must be given the opportunity to add value in a way that they will find rewarding, which fits their talents and highest values, such as the arts or sports, *and* link this activity to wealth creation and preservation. Although it is always great to hand over the family business to the next generation, it is more important to ensure that you never let your family cloud your judgement. The business must be placed in the hands of the most capable people who may not necessarily be your bloodline.

It is important to understand and appreciate that every human being strives for self-actualisation. However, the form this takes will vary according to their wealth generation, as shown below.

First Generation: Survival Mode

They have come from nothing, so their immediate needs are to survive and then build a wealth platform so that their children can avoid going through a similar experience.

The first generation may not know that their story should never be forgotten over the course of time; instead, it should act as an inspiration for future generations. So why is this not documented?

This *rags-to-riches* story should be recorded and retained as an asset for the family, as it forms an essential part of the family's intellectual and human capital. Questions that should be asked and not forgotten would include: *where did they come from, what was life like growing up without wealth and how was their financial success achieved?*

This human capital element is just as valuable to the family as any financial planning that the family undertakes. Their story acts as a lesson in life that will help future generations to understand and appreciate where they have come from and the importance of the family name.

Unfortunately, the first generation, because of their life experiences, will have different values and appreciation of money. It should never be assumed that the next generation will *think and feel the same way about finance*; after all, they have never experienced a life *without* money!

As such, the first generation should avoid enforcing their values on wealth onto the next generations, as this can and will cause emotional conflict.

Second Generation: Sustain

Unlike the previous generation, they have never had to *work to eat* so their survival instincts are not inbuilt. However, they have experienced first-hand the *growing* success of their parents.

The onus here is on *sustaining* and *building on* the platform created by their parents.

Usually, at least one child continues to work in the family business that has been started by their parents. This may or may not be out of choice, as it is more often of a sign of respect to the first-generation parent. Remember: 70% of families will lose *all* their wealth within two generations – both history and statistics indicate that your family is doomed to fail financially unless you take the relevant action.

It is also important to never assume that the second generation will always follow in the footsteps of the first generation by taking over the family business.

Take John D. Rockefeller, Jr., who was the sole heir to the Rockefeller fortune, as an example. He resigned from the family business with his father's blessing to focus on his philanthropic interests. By donating over $537 million in his lifetime, including a land donation in New York to the UN, where their headquarters are now based, he established the family name and helped to grow an extensive network of social, political connections and institutional power that his father began and his children continued.

Third Generation and Beyond: Struggle and Loss

The fact that they have been given everything in life -- creates different problems because they will struggle to find their role in life.

If they continue to feel unimportant or lack purpose, they will seek immediate gratification and dopamine fixes, such as alcohol, drugs and gambling. This can be avoided if the third generation is supported through effective communication in their search for happiness and purpose. However, it is crucial that the path they follow is linked to wealth preservation and self-sustainability.

Let's look at an example to support this point.

If the third generation wants to pursue a career in music, what should the family do? Do they simply put down this idea and force the individual to work in the family business instead because it's in the best interests of everyone other than the person in question?

Quite clearly, this will create resistance that leads to anger and resentment. On the other hand, do you blindly fund their pursuit of a career in music without seeking to see if the interest is genuine and they are willing to work towards their dream and goal?

The answer lies in a happy medium.

If the person is genuinely interested and passionate about creating a career in music, then they will do what it takes to make this a success because they are following the path they have chosen and love. Nobody will have to force or motivate them to practice and work on their music.

Therefore, the initial idea or concept should be tested.

If they are genuine, they will have no issue in working from the bottom within the music world to learn and understand what it takes to become a success in their musical field. Even more importantly, they should have no problems working in the family business to make the money that is required to self-fund their dream.

Giving money without the recipient earning it will never create or establish an appreciation of making money; therefore, this must be avoided wherever possible.

Andrew Carnegie, the steel magnate who was the richest man on the planet at the time, wrote in 1899 that leaving large fortunes to your heirs was *misguided affection* because *great sums bequeathed often work more for the injury than the good of the recipients.*

The way we live our lives depends on the *hierarchy of needs* (as expressed by Maslow).

It is imperative that rather than judge the members of our family, we should embrace and appreciate their values. Quite simply, emotion causes conflict and conflict costs money.

If conflict is to be avoided, then the right balance

should be reached by supporting the values of all the family members whilst avoiding simply giving money away.

As an example of how values work, a mother who places the highest value on her family will always ensure that the wellbeing of her children is her highest priority. If her husband values finance most highly, he would make investing, business and finance his top priority.

If the mother judged her husband on her values, she would consider him to be an irresponsible father for regularly working late, but the husband would think that he was a brilliant family man for working so hard to provide for his family. The two different perceptions of the same situation will cause conflict and a potential break-up if they are not dealt with through effective communication.

In his bestselling book, *Family Wealth,* James E. Hughes, Jr. stated that: "I believe the father's willingness to free his son to follow his individual pursuit of happiness is one of the best long-term wealth preservation decisions in history."

Today, more than 120 years since the founding of their fortune, the Rockefeller family clearly understands that its wealth lies in its human and intellectual capital. Its financial capital has become a tool to enhance its individual members' pursuit of happiness. They have successfully got the right balance between business, investing and using philanthropy to enhance the family name, as well as its social and political connections.

Emotions DO Cost Money

*"If you cannot control your emotions
don't expect to control your money."*
Warren Buffett

Having spoken to and interviewed over 400 business owners and property investors, I found that something kept repeating itself – *emotions cost money!*

What does that mean?

Quite simply, when one makes decisions that are based on the heart rather than the mind, all thoughts of financial realism are virtually forgotten.

For example, do you remember when you purchased your family home? When you made that decision, did you use emotions or logic? Did the property require renovation, and if so, did you go over budget because you wanted to create the house that you loved?

Another example is divorce, where emotions will leave only the lawyers as the outright winners!

In a family environment, emotional relationships can either make or break a family.

The failure to appreciate everyone's values within the family will inevitably cause conflict. Emotional conflict may lead to family breakdown and that can cause financial failure and usually will.

Clear concise communication that is connected to a system — the family governance — may be difficult to implement, but it is key to your family's long-term success.

Exploring how this can be done should be at the heart of sound, effective personal and family wealth management.

2. Establishing a Family Vision

If it is done correctly, documenting the *family vision* will act as an inspiration for all future generations and create both value and meaning to the family name. A family may not be a business, but it should, in certain cases, *act like on*e if it is serious about creating a wealth legacy that will flourish for over a century.

I call this *the business of being a family.*

It is essential that this process is fun and involving. This is not a business plan that has to be *correct* the first time around. Instead, it is an evolving process that will bring your family closer together *and* provide them with a better understanding of the importance of the family name.

A family needs to be treated like a business if it is to successfully maintain and grow its wealth over multiple generations, and every successful business is aligned with a single documented vision.

What is this vision?

Quite simply, it is an expression of the purpose,

values and goals of the family. The creation of a family vision statement is the starting point that will lead to your family becoming sufficiently organised to preserve its wealth. If you cannot define your vision, how will you know what your investment, planning and action priorities are?

> "If you fail to plan then you plan to fail."
> **Dr John Demartini**

What are the key areas that any family vision statement should cover? It should:

- Help to provide a clear understanding of the family's purpose.

- Define the common vision of the family.

- Express the values that the family shares.

- Acknowledge any secrets that the family has – this will create trust and openness amongst *all* the family members.

- Provide the history of the family, told as a series of stories – this will be the glue that binds the family together.

- Be the form of governance that the family wishes to follow, which will help to grow the family wealth in the long term.

- Provide a clear explanation of everyone's role within the family, which effectively explains each individual member's mission within the family vision.

You should also ensure that every family member has a role within the family. No one should be deemed as an outcast because this will inevitably cause resentment.

3. Aligning Your Professional Power Team To The Family Vision

Usually, the main entrepreneurial member(s) of the family will have built the family wealth with the assistance of their *professional power team*. Such a team may include the following:

- Lawyers – which could be from more than one practice.

- Accountants – such as for the family business and for each individual.

- Tax advisors.

- Bankers – those that provide funding on projects and investments.

- Financial Advisors – those that control the family's funds and investments.

- Trustees – if assets are held in Trust.

- Fiduciary companies – they tend to maintain offshore structures.

We always advocate creating a *professional* power team, and we also think it is vital that the family vision is communicated clearly to that team. After all, how can they advise you on how to achieve your goals if they do not know what your goals are?

The biggest mistake that any family or business can ever make is to expect their professional advisors to *guess* what the family wishes are.

Successful businesses hold regular Board meetings with directors and key personnel.

Why do they do this?

Quite simply, to ensure that the objectives of the business can be clearly communicated and reviewed amongst their key decision makers.

Does it not make sense to hold a similar meeting with your professional advisors?

Not only will this make them accountable to you on a regular basis, but more importantly, encourage them to communicate with one another. This will ensure that the family mission and goals are clearly understood and aligned with the advice being provided.

This leads very nicely to my next point...

4. Make Sure That The Next Generation Feel At Ease With Their Professional Power Team

Meetings with all professional advisors can be a daunting experience as they tend to be very serious and not much fun.

From a control point of view, the person who has set up and built the professional team (usually the first wealth creator of the family), tends to maintain the relationship with these advisors and does *not* share it with his family. These factors can cause splits between the family members (especially the next generation) and the professional team that has been assigned to look after their requirements, leading to isolation.

Creating a situation where the family is dependent on just one person is a big risk that can affect the family's financial future. So, make sure that more than one person within the family takes the responsibility of understanding how the family's wealth is structured.

There is no point creating complex offshore structures and then only allowing one person to understand how and why they have been created. After all, what will happen to the family's wealth if that person suddenly loses mental capacity or passes away?

We recently worked with a family whose assets were held in various offshore companies set up by the father. Unfortunately, he never took the time to explain the details of these complex offshore structures to another family member and so it took over four years after he passed away to resolve the *puzzle* that he had created.

Quite simply, this is a *huge* risk which needs to be recognised and resolved simply because it can be very expensive to fix.

It is much simpler to educate or at least introduce additional family members to the professional team. This will not only empower the family member(s), but also create a rapport and understanding with the family's professional power team.

Making introductions during one's lifetime is simple and very cost-effective, and creating a document, such as a Lasting Power of Attorney, is a very simple way to prevent family assets and bank accounts from being potentially frozen!

It is also very important to understand that you can control your assets without having direct ownership, and that simply transferring the ownership of assets to the next generation will leave them open to the risk of loss via any of the following:

- Divorce – assets will not pass down the bloodline
- Poor financial decision making – is the next generation qualified to make sound financial decisions?
- Bankruptcy – the assets will be lost to creditors
- Litigation

The concept of controlling assets without having direct ownership is crucial to wealth retention and asset protection within a family and this is something that should be communicated with your professional power team.

5. Effective Communication

Before you read any further, can you appreciate why effective communication would need to be included in this list?

We meet people who agree that effective communication is great idea ... *for someone else's family!* And it can be hard for successful people to acknowledge that their personal communication skills could improve. But we are talking about improving your own personal communication skills *and* the communication style within the family.

Imagine a Executive Board scenario where people dominate proceedings or withhold information. Karl George wrote a bestselling book, *The Effective Board Member* that explains the consequences when board members are deficient in their communication.

Effective communication covers:

- Communication with the power team – make sure the team both understands and are accountable to the family's vision and wishes.

- Your progeny needs to totally understand the structure that you've set up and why.

- Any sibling rivalry conflicts should be handled *now* in order to avoid expensive litigation fees in the future and the inevitable breakdown of the family that would follow. Ironically, silence causes conflict because it can lead to assumptions being made that can escalate, yet it can easily be avoided by confronting the issue(s) with the relevant party through effective communication.

The main reason for conflict and failure within the family is poor communication or at least a lack of good quality communication within the family structure. This will lead to various differing family values not being appreciated. This, in turn, will lead to miscommunication, which may lead to emotional anger and inevitably cost money!

Let's look back at my earlier example of the family-run construction business worth approximately £1 billion.

The father failed to explain to his two surviving sons what his intentions were for the business and for the family wealth, as well as his reasons why the money and the assets would be divided between them. Instead, he assumed that by splitting everything equally between them in his Will, everything would be OK.

His failure to properly communicate his wishes and thoughts to his children about the future of the business and the legacy of the wealth caused his family, and the wealth that he had created, to self-implode.

Ensuring that the family regularly communicates will avoid future conflict. This includes not just regular communication within the family, but also with the family's professional advisors.

Make sure that all the advisors clearly understand the family's needs and wishes and make them accountable at all times. After all, their job – for which they are being paid very well – is to serve the best interests of the family and not to maximise their fees.

It is important to note that lawyers (and accountants, to some extent) who charge an hourly rate have a conflict of interest. Why?

Quite simply because they will earn more if there is a conflict within the family that leads to litigation.

Therefore, the onus is on you - the family - to avoid emotional conflict, ensure effective communication between you all and get all the professional advisors on board. It is also vital that more than one person within the family has a working relationship with all the family advisors and this needs to be maintained.

Finally, a failure to understand the human and intellectual capital that exists within the family environment can lead to emotional conflict. What do we mean by this? Most families believe that financial planning is the most important means of maintaining their wealth and, subsequently, of passing it through the family. Although financial planning is important, it is NOT the most important aspect of wealth retention.

For example, the main wealth creator (usually the first generation wealth) will focus on preparing a will in order for the assets to be passed down to the next generation. If these families are savvy, they will get the right tax advice to ensure that the assets are passed down in a tax-efficient manner.

Whilst it is important to have a tax-efficient will, what use is it if the detail within it is not communicated to the family members during the lifetime of the donor? Questions, such as why the assets have been transferred and to whom, and who is left in charge to run the business(es), need to be discussed in a conversation during the donor's lifetime. They are certainly not questions the lifetime beneficiaries should have to guess the answers to!

Unfortunately, far too many family disputes are caused because conversations about wills are kept secret. This can even break up the family permanently because the subject matter needs to be discussed during the donor's lifetime.

Why risk future litigation amongst your family? Your legacy and that of your family must be both planned and arranged during your lifetime and not delayed until after your death.

6. Get The Next Generation To Understand and Appreciate Wealth

The next generation should be educated that money is difficult to earn and very easy to lose. We have already highlighted this by looking at historical financial mistakes and how easy it is for the family's entire wealth to be lost, regardless of the amount of money involved. There are many examples given below and this is not an exhaustive list!

- Divorce – but this can be avoided if the assets are not directly owned by family members, as per point 5 above

- Poor investment decisions and failed enterprises

- Being ripped off by advisors and so-called experts

- Lawsuits

- Family Conflicts

- Overindulgent spending – this is spending more than you earn. This proved to be the downfall of the Vanderbilt family, who now only have a legacy of philanthropy

- Taking on too much debt – such as Patricia Kluge and the Stroh family.

- Giving it away to charity – although philanthropy can be vital in sustaining the family name, it is essential to realise that not all charities can be supported. In fact, the decision to give money to support a charity should be treated in the same way as investing money in a business.
  The following questions should be asked first before donating substantial sums:
  - Who are the charity's trustees?
  - Do they have a financial background?
  - Does the charity have ideas or procedures in place
  to be self-sustaining or will they require money every year?
  - How will the charity spend its donations?

Having a good education in finance, business and investing will help you to reduce the risk of family wealth being lost to such persons and scenarios.

Going back to the original point, a question that can cause great pain for most families is: *"Do my children appreciate and value wealth?"*

There are several ways that parents can ground their children. Examples include:

- Giving your children the opportunity to accept and experience working and earning the right to wealth.

- Giving your children the opportunity to add value in a way that they will find rewarding, which fits their talents and highest values.

- Empowering your children to understand finance and investing – this may be done with the help of a mentor.

- Set up a family bank that is established purely for the purpose of making lending decisions to investments or business ideas that individual family members may have.

- Establish a philanthropic arm of the family. This should contain a 'Board' of family members who are genuinely interested in philanthropy and can collectively make informed decisions on any charity they may decide to support. An entity can also be established to ensure that such donations are done in the most tax-efficient manner.

Lifestyle Vision

Understanding the vision for your *lifestyle.*

Any wealth strategy that you put into place has to complement the lifestyle vision of each individual family member.

What is a person's *lifestyle?* It is understanding what you want your day to look and feel like.

So ask yourself: *how do you want to live your life?*

In order to live a fulfilled life, your lifestyle must match your highest values.

7. Get An External Mentor And Trustee For Both The Family And The Next Generation

If you try and mentor your own children you are limited by the fact that you are in the equation. This is why it is important to get an external mentor from outside the family. The mentor that you should be looking for is someone who understands the concept of family and applies or can apply the principles already mentioned.

What Is A Mentor?

A mentor is the central part of the teaching nucleus of the family. They must be in a position of respect and trust. More importantly they need to be able to create a two-way learning bond with their chosen mentee. They act as a guide by challenging your goals, debating your ideas and helping you to learn from past mistakes and deal with failure if it arises.

Great mentors will assist the mentee, through a series of questions, to arrive at the optimum answer.

Learning via a mentor must always be bespoke to the requirements laid out by the mentee.

Being without a mentor is like trying a new sport without a coach. You may learn about the sport through books and videos but ultimately when you go out to play, especially in a competitive environment, you will probably fail!

What Is A Trustee?

In the realms of the family dynamic a Trustee is an independent third party who acts as an impartial guide and advisor for all the family members. As the name suggests they come from a position of trust and it is crucial that they can be approached unconditionally.

This role is not to be confused with the generic term for Trustee which tends to be a person or group of persons who are responsible for the management and maintenance of assets that have been settled into a Trust. The Family Trustee is responsible for the man-agement and maintenance of the family's intellectual and human capital by acting as a confidant and media-tor for the entire family.

It is vital that the Family Trustee has no ulterior motive other than the success and well-being of the family and its members. It is not unusual for the Family Trustee to also be a mentor to the family's leaders.

Not surprisingly, both mentors and trustees would need to declare any *conflict of interest* as and when it is known.

This might require them to step down from that capacity.

We have also found that the mentor and trustee role works more effectively if they are guided by four fundamentals, to follow.

PART 2: THE FOUR FUNDAMENTALS OF FAMILY PROSPERITY

The Problem With Traditional Professional Services

We have so far discussed how wealth can be lost within the family and the various risks that cause 90% of families to lose all their wealth within three generations. We hope you agree that the amount of money your family has is irrelevant when it comes to avoiding financial failure and becoming another sad statistic.

You are never too big to fail!

We have also provided various examples of families who have lost it all, despite their large fortunes.

The reality is that *traditional professional services* will *not* prevent your family from becoming one of the 90% that lose all their wealth within two or three generations. The most detailed study in the area of family wealth, which was undertaken by the *Williams Group*, highlighted the real reasons why families lose all their wealth (known as post-transition failure).

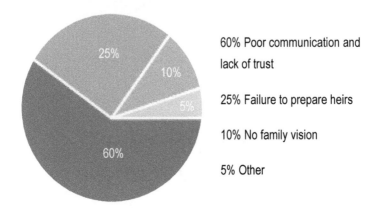

60% Poor communication and lack of trust

25% Failure to prepare heirs

10% No family vision

5% Other

Therefore, despite 95% of financial failure being caused *within the family*, nearly all traditional advisors continue to focus their efforts on servicing the area that causes only 5% of financial failure, which is financial, wealth and tax planning!

Clearly, families need advice that is bespoke to their needs and deals with the *whole* family rather than focusing on one or two key decision makers.

We have created a prototypical model to help summarise what is required to sustain, protect and grow the family's wealth over multiple generations; essentially, securing long-term family prosperity.

Although we have highlighted the seven key areas in this report, these can be grouped together to what we call the four fundamentals of family prosperity.

The Four Fundamentals Of Family Prosperity

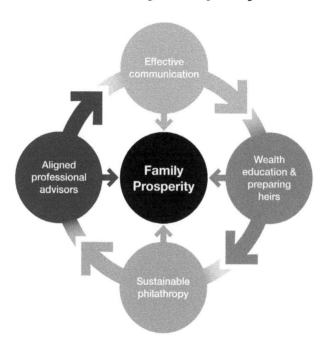

The Four Fundamentals of Family Prosperity

Just like the four wheels of a car, if any one of these four components are missing, historical data suggests that your family's future wealth and prosperity will dissipate.

It is important to note that not only do they follow a cycle, but they interact and cross-reference the other elements mutually; and *all* impact family prosperity.

If any of the fundamentals are not implemented, then we can infer that you family will be one of the 90% that lose all their wealth within three generations!

Let us explore the four fundamentals.

1. Effective Communication: The Foundation Of Family Prosperity

When you build a house, it is vital that you have solid foundations; otherwise, it will collapse. It is exactly the same with family prosperity.

Communication is vital as it enhances trust within the family. If it is done effectively, it will avoid destructive and expensive behaviour, such as litigation and divorce.

So why do families fail to build these solid foundations by providing and encouraging excellent lines of communication, both internally within the family and externally with their professional advisors? Why do families essentially *bury their heads in the sand?*

This was a question that we struggled to answer ourselves. Maybe families do not understand the problem or the issue at hand, maybe they are not being advised correctly or maybe they think the problems can be resolved over time without any effort. The answer is actually a combination of all the above that we call *Normality Bias.*

Normality bias (or *normalcy bias*) - or, as we prefer to call it, *burying your head in the sand* - is a mental state that people enter when they face a disaster. It causes people to underestimate both the possibility of a disaster and its possible effects because it causes people to have a bias to believe that things will always function the way they normally do.

Essentially, if a disaster has *never* occurred before then it will *never* occur.

In the case of family wealth, if families are *currently wealthy* then the consensus is that they will *always be wealthy*. However, research has proven that this is not the case. The other problem with normalcy bias is that it can result in an inability to cope with a disaster once it occurs.

Clearly, if the family wants to thrive over multiple generations, normalcy bias within a family dynamic must be dealt with. The first step is to build solid foundations by establishing clear and effective communication. This will inevitably build trust between all the family members.

Two Parts To Effective Communication

Effective communication should be divided into two parts – *internal communication* and *external communication* - and we shall take both parts in turn.

Internal Communication

This is communication *within* the family.

Essentially, it allows all members to fully understand each other's values and intentions. If this is done effectively, it will build both trust and rapport amongst family members.

If this is not done, or done badly, then members will create their own stories and conclusions about the family wealth and each member's intentions.

It will also lead to distrust, conflict and a divided family which will cause litigation, divorce and even behavioural and addiction issues for some family members.

An Expensive Litigation Nightmare

A real-life example of how this can go wrong is with one of our clients who we shall call M (her real name will be protected as we provide extreme confidentiality to all our clients).

M has only one sibling, but the lack of regular consistent family communication with their parents when they were alive has now resulted in the two siblings taking legal action against one another over the assets and wealth left to them by their father. This has destroyed the family relationship and cost millions of pounds in legal fees.

It was a shame that the *Charles Group* was never drafted in to resolve the family's communication issues when both parents were alive because we would have saved both siblings a substantial amount of money in legal fees, and they would have had a working, social relationship today.

In this scenario, do you really think that this was the situation that their parents wanted for their only two children? Of course, they didn't!

Their father (first generation) worked for over 40 years to provide for his two children, yet his legacy was that the wealth was lost on lawyers to support the destructive litigation.

Can We Help?

We strongly recommend that our clients implement many practical communication solutions to ensure that the family regularly and effectively communicates across generations and, of course, we can help with this.

Solutions include well-structured formal family meetings that help to establish the family's vision, regular family roundtable events that are fun, and the capturing of important family video messages that are then kept.

Having this effective communication will enable families to take a multi-generational approach to managing their investments, trusts and philanthropic activities.

By taking such an approach, senior family members will help younger members to understand how effective wealth management supports the family's near-term financial goals and long-term wealth preservation. More importantly, effective communication builds trust and a sense of purpose that will help family members to work together to achieve the family vision. It also ensures that the human and intellectual capital, and not just the wealth, is passed down across generations.

The Rockefellers

The value of human and intellectual capital should never be underestimated as, in most cases, it is worth more (albeit intangibly) than the family's physical wealth.

A great example of how this has worked effectively is the Rockefeller family. John D Rockefeller Sr., who at the time was one of America's wealthiest men, did not obligate his only son to remain in the family business, but allowed him to follow his own calling instead, which was in family governance and philanthropy.

In this instance, his willingness to free his only son and allow him to follow his individual pursuit of happiness is one of the best long-term wealth preservation decisions in history.

What is even more interesting is the fact that John D Rockefeller Jr., urged each of his children to find work that led to their individual pursuit of happiness.

The resulting contributions of the third generation of Rockefellers to philanthropy, government, international banking and investment in new industries has been remarkable.

Today, more than 120 years since the founding of the fortune, the Rockefeller family clearly understands that its wealth lies in its human and intellectual capital and that its financial capital is a tool to enhance the pursuits of happiness of its individual members. They are a family that understands the importance of having regular and effective communication within the family.

External Communication

This is communication between the family and its *external* advisors. Professional advisors come in multiple forms but would generally include, but not limited to the following:

- Your accountant

- Your lawyer

- Your tax advisors

- Your investment advisors

- Your private bank managers

- Your trustees

- Your mortgage brokers
- Your fund managers
- Other

Although they may be great at what they do in their own specialist field, this does not necessarily mean they are working well as a collective unit. In fact, it is not unusual for one advisor to offer advice that contradicts what another has said.

For example, legal advice may be given without any regard to the tax consequences or tax advice provided without considering its commercial effect.

Even the reviewing of existing structures and agreements, such as wills to ensure they are up to date and meet the families *current* objectives, is often overlooked. For example, we reviewed a family will that did not account for the person's change of country of residence!

It is, therefore, important that the following questions are asked when you are assessing how effective your existing communication is with current advisors. After all, if you are not regularly communicating with your advisors, how can you expect them to effectively service your requirements?

- Do they KNOW your requirements? Has the family vision been created and then communicated to your advisors?

- Who within the family is responsible for communicating with the family advisors? Does this responsibility rest with one person or is it shared by several family members?

- Do all the adult members of your family know the family advisors, or have they, at the very least, met them?

- How often do you meet with your advisors? Regularly or sporadically? Are you being proactive or reactively waiting for a disaster to happen before you meet with your advisors?

- How often, if at all, do you meet with ALL your advisors in one meeting? You will be surprised that the whole (all of your advisors) can solve problems, where the previous advisors acting alone could not. Such a meeting will ensure that your advisors are working collectively to help achieve your family's vision.
The whole is greater than the sum of the parts.

We had a classic case where one family implemented tax advice but failed to effectively communicate the desired outcome with their advisors.

They thought they wanted *Inheritance Tax* advice, but what they actually wanted was a *tax-efficient method* of giving money to some of the children, whilst giving ownership of the business to the other children who were running it daily with their father.

Although the inheritance tax advice was very good, it failed to fulfil what the family wanted and caused family disunity.

Review of Communication In The Practical World

The most successful companies in the world all have the same thing in common:

- They have a Board of Directors – with each Board member being given a precise role within the company (e.g. Marketing Director, Finance Director and Chief Executive Officer).

- The Board meets regularly to discuss the company's vision, how the company has progressed over a period of time and what the company needs to do before the next meeting.

Does your family do the same? Does each member have a designated role to ensure that the family's wealth will be successfully preserved for multiple generations?

How often do you meet up as a family to formally discuss the progress of each member and the family as a whole?

If your family does not formally meet up at least once per annum, then there will be a high risk of financial failure because communication is the foundation of family wealth. In fact, we would recommend that your family formally meets once per quarter.

It should be remembered that your family is a business – the business of multi-generational wealth preservation and the business of being a family. Therefore, your family needs to implement certain ideologies of businesses if it is to succeed, starting with the creation of a formal board of family members. As the family grows, it should end up with a structure that looks like this:

- Family Board
- Family Committee
- Family Assembly

Family Board – with similar roles to a corporate board of directors

The Family Board will run the day-to-day activities of the family. Each member is given specific roles within the family. The Board needs to meet on a regular basis at least once a quarter in order to discuss progress and all of the key important issues. This Board should consist of direct family members, such as the father, mother and children.

Family Committee – the members act like shareholders of a company

They are responsible for voting on all major issues that are highlighted by the Board, as well as voting on how the Board is formed and who will be re-elected to remain on the Board. This committee should meet at least once every six months or when the Board requires something urgent to be voted on. Members can include the children's spouses and aunties and uncles.

The Family Assembly

This is essentially the remaining family members, as well as those included in the assembly and on the Board. Their role is to simply attend an annual meeting/gala of all family members to get an update on the family's progress.

2. Wealth Education And Preparing The Heirs

This will help the heirs or the next generation to be prepared to receive the wealth, and more importantly, appreciate the wealth that they are to receive. Wealth education sits outside of the traditional education that most people can expect to receive. It includes, but is not limited to, financial education, mentoring and being groomed to take over the existing family business.

It prepares the heirs - or the next generation - to be prepared to receive the wealth - and more importantly - to appreciate the wealth they are to receive.

Why is it so critical?

According to social affairs journalist, May Bulman (2018), adults from England are amongst the worst performers on basic, everyday numeracy task like working out the change they should receive from a shopping trip!

An extensive joint study by the University College of London (UCL) and the University of Cambridge showed that four in ten could not apply a simple discount to an everyday household product they might buy at a supermarket.

An adult survey that asked simple questions such as *What is tax?* and *Where does tax come from?* showed a disturbing number of adults have no idea that *they pay tax!*

The survey showed that 12% of most 15 years olds could answer basic financial questions correctly. On average, 22% had only basic financial literacy.

Finance blogger Max Rofagha says a *PWC* survey (2017) of 5,500 *millennials* aged 18-28 found that only 24% could demonstrate basic financial knowledge.

The conclusion of the survey was that almost half of working adults currently have financial literacy skills we'd expect of primary school aged children.

MyBnk.org claims that young adults have credit card debts of £3,000 and more people 30 plus are struggling to pay household bills.

They conclude, 50% of students in academies, sixth forms, colleges and free and independent schools are not required to be taught money skills.

In 2018, over 250 plus organisations in the UK were engaged in teaching *adults* financial literacy.

Given the above, it's likely that some of your family members might not yet be ready to assume the responsibility of making prudent financial decisions.

This is why they need financial education and mentoring.

Financial Education

This involves understanding money and how it works; more importantly, it provides an appreciation of money itself. Amazingly, this is not usually taught as part of a *regular education*, even though everyone at some stage in their lives will receive, earn and spend money.

Financial education is an essential part of preparing the heirs of your family, which can be taught in person, learnt or a combination of both. There are many excellent books that have been written on the subject, although we would also recommend the appointment of a mentor. If the next generation is not taught how to value money, how can you expect them to retain and grow the wealth for the following generation?

Mentorship

Mentors should be an essential part of the family's team of advisors. Anyone in the family can be mentored, provided they are willing and ready to learn. A mentor acts as a guide who asks great questions so that the mentee can gain a better understanding of both themselves and the relevant subject. Unlike teachers, mentors never provide answers. Instead, they seek to provide mentees with the questions that will best lead to learning.

There are many definitions of mentorship which can cause confusion, but we have decided that the best one is expressed by B Bozeman and MK Feeney in their book, *Toward a Useful Theory of Mentoring.*

'Mentoring is a process for the informal transmission of knowledge, social capital, and the psychosocial support perceived by the recipient as relevant to work, career, or professional development; mentoring entails informal communication, usually face to face and during a sustained period of time, between a person who is perceived to have greater knowledge, wisdom or experience (the mentor) and a person who is perceived to have less (the mentee or protégé).'

A successful mentor provides a learning process that is unique to the protégé and can be used throughout their lifetime.

True mentorship is the expression of wisdom through intuition that guides someone towards greater self-awareness and freedom in their pursuit of happiness. It should not be just restricted to finance and wealth as a great mentor who uses learning methods unique to their protégé, will enhance the life skills that are necessary for the retention and growth of the family wealth.

A mentor should not be mistaken for a teacher, elder or best friend, although these people can act as mentors as well if they are called upon to form such a relationship.

Grooming The Next Generation
To Take Over The Business

Family businesses always have a sense of attachment and emotional connection. It is understandable that the first generation will have a sense of pride over their achievement in both starting and developing a successful business. However, unless the intention is to sell the business, then a clear and concise succession plan will need to be implemented.

Unfortunately, too many family businesses leave succession to chance (sometimes only leaving the next generation to take over when the first generation dies), or even worse, they rush the process.

It should never be assumed that business and leadership skills are simply a matter of genetics, as merely being the child of a successful businessperson does not automatically mean that you will be great at doing business.

It is a process that needs to be learned.

In fact, you should not assume that the next generation will have an interest in taking over the reins of the business. Remember John D Rockefeller Junior; in his pursuit of happiness, he chose to follow philanthropy rather than take over the phenomenal company that his father had built.

For any succession to be a success, it is vital that the next generation is given both the time and support that is required to learn their way around the business.

An out of touch new owner who has not been seen to have paid their dues is unlikely to endear themselves to the employees, the existing Board of Directors or the other shareholders.

An ill-prepared new owner will also lead to incapable management and potentially disastrous decisions which can, and often will, affect the future of the business.

Generational transfers are complicated and should not be left to chance. Not only do the tax and legal consequences need to be considered, but also the future of the company will be dependent on the succession plan. Will the new owner be ready and have earned the right to take over the business? Have they earned the respect of their peers and company employees, and more importantly, do they want to succeed their parents in the business or have they simply been pushed into a role that's based on their surname? These are all fundamental questions that must be answered during the succession process.

A clear, organised succession plan often goes a long way towards smoothing the rocky transitional period.

Parents should look to give their children incrementally increasing responsibility and control. It is a delicate balancing act and the parents' role is critical to this process. If they let control go too quickly, they could very rapidly see the family business slide into oblivion, but if there is too much meddling, they will risk denting whatever self-belief their children might have in leaving a positive mark on the business.

Five Factors to Consider When You're Creating a Successful Succession Plan and Structuring the Family Business

The following simply highlights the key areas that need to be considered before introducing a member of the family and/or spouses into the family business.

1. Ensure The Family Member Has *Earned* The Right To Their Role

Simply being born from the *correct womb* does not give you the immediate right to obtain a high-ranking, high salary position within the family business. Assess the family member's current skills, experience and expertise and then give them a position that is justified, based on these criteria.

Personally, I would recommend that they gain experience by initially working for a business in a similar industry. This will avoid any chance of favouritism, whilst at the same time giving the person the required knowledge and sense of personal achievement.

If the person wants to start immediately in the family business, then they can, but it should only be at the bottom and they should only be given the same opportunities as every other employee.

2. Don't Create Two Classes of Employees

Your business will inevitably depend on non-family members. It is therefore critical to treat everyone equally when it comes to hiring, salary, benefits and opportunities for growth.

Special treatment to family members, or even the perception of this, will demotivate employees and create tension. Following on from point 1, one should never put your family members on the payroll if they cannot make a real contribution to the business.

3. Put It In Writing – A Family Business Agreement

Quite simply, a handshake is *not* enough, especially when family members must protect and care for their children, spouses and estates.

A family business agreement provides legal protection and serves as a guiding document. If this is done from the outset, it will remove any future emotional conflicts that nearly always end up in very expensive and destructive litigation. The areas that need to be discussed and included in any agreement will be the salary and dividend pay-outs, the expected work schedule of everyone, as well as responsibilities and commitment.

How will big decisions be made? What happens if someone wants to sell the company, can no longer work or gets divorced?

These may be uncomfortable conversations for the family, but it's better to have them early on when there are fewer emotions and less stress involved.

Like all agreements, it will need to be reviewed and updated every year as people's personal circumstances are forever changing.

4. Put Something In Place to Protect The Family Business From Disaster

Unfortunately, life is unpredictable, so it is essential that nothing is left to chance.

We would recommend having a written agreement to determine what happens to the family business in the event of a disability or death of one or more family members. You should also complement this with insurance to provide cover if any of the *key persons* of the business pass away.

Any agreement must be made binding on third parties, as well as the heirs and relatives.

Like all agreements, it is essential that the key points are effectively communicated to all the family members to avoid any potential future disputes. This agreement would need to be reviewed and updated every year.

5. Separate Family And Business Time

The stress of running a business can wreak havoc on relationships. Good quality family time is essential as it promotes effective communication, which plays a vital role in both sustaining and growing the family's wealth for multiple generations.

Therefore, create some rules that will stop people talking about business during *family time*, such as dinners or family vacations.

Creating and sustaining the family business isn't right for all family members but it can be fulfilling. Just remember, however, that the health of your business and the relationship with your family will rely on regular and effective communication with *all* your family members, not just those that are in the business.

3. Sustainable Philanthropy

If we look at the world's most successful families, such as the Rockefellers, Waltons and Mars, it is clear that they all have one thing in common – a sustainable philanthropic arm.

Further evidence of this can be seen in the 2015 survey conducted by EY and Kennesaw State University of the world's largest family businesses, *Staying power: how do family businesses create lasting success?* The results highlighted the importance of philanthropy by revealing that:

- 81% of the world's largest family businesses practice philanthropy

- Their giving is almost equally split between charitable giving and service to the community

- 47% have a family foundation

- 37% had plans to increase their philanthropic contributions during the year and 62% had plans to give at the same level.

So why is philanthropy so important for your family?

Andrew Carnegie, who was the richest man in the world and at the forefront of charitable giving, took it to the extreme by donating his entire wealth to philanthropic causes before he passed away:

"The man who dies thus rich dies disgraced. Such, in my opinion, is the true gospel concerning wealth, obedience to which is destined someday to solve the problem of the rich and the poor. Wealth is not to feed our egos but to feed the hungry and to help people help themselves."

Andrew Carnegie

Whilst we would not advise you to give your entire estate away, it is vital for your family to have a purpose that is greater than the individual wants and needs of each family member.

The only way to achieve this is to establish a philanthropic arm that unites and inspires the whole family.

Philanthropy should not be solely used to create public goodwill for the family and business opportunities for the family business, although it will inevitably create these opportunities.

Also, creating a family foundation can have several tax advantages, yet none of these reasons should be the key driver when you're establishing a sustainable philanthropic arm for the family. Giving must be authentic, inspirational, and but most importantly, unite all the family members.

The key benefits of setting up a sustainable philanthropic arm for the family's wealth are as follows:

1. A philanthropic arm, that is consistent with the family's vision, demonstrates the family's core values.

2. It unites all the family members to a common goal, which is important because not all of them will be directly involved in the family business and investment dealings.

3. It enables every family member to have a meaningful contribution to family financial decisions.

4. It inspires all family members to work together to ensure that the family wealth will not just survive, but also thrive for multiple generations, as you will all have a cause that's much greater than just the family members wealthy livelihoods.

5. Sustainable philanthropy enables the family to use their wealth to make a significant difference to the world that we live in today. Whilst this may seem altruistic, it will have great benefits for the family, such as creating both huge public goodwill for the family name and great connections with society, as well as providing increased popularity and business opportunities for the family business.

What is Sustainable Philanthropy?

Deciding on what charitable causes the family donates its money to should be like making an investment in a business.

Whilst one is not necessarily looking for a return on one's investment, it is important to establish how well the charity is run, how experienced the Board of Trustees are, how much money goes to the charitable cause and how much is *lost* through administrative expenses. You do not want to be in a situation that occurred when the *Kids Company*, a UK charity, collapsed despite receiving over £46m in public funding. These risks can, of course, be overcome by setting up your own family charitable trust, although that will give rise to other issues.

Sustainable philanthropy is essentially the ability to be self-sufficient and secure repeated income whilst at the same time efficiently controlling the costs so that the causes being supported receive the maximum amount of donations.

You can also be smart with the way that you make donations. For example, rather than simply sending a charity money, it may be better to donate shares to them with a deed that stipulates that it cannot sell the shares (unless this is done in agreement with the donor and / or their family) but receive all the shares' dividends instead. This means the charity can rely on the continuous income that will be derived from the shares whilst also benefiting from the capital growth of those shares.

Another example would be to donate a rental

property to a charity and stipulate that the charity cannot sell the asset but receive all the rental income instead.

To summarise sustainable philanthropy, it is essential to remember the following:

- Choose a charitable cause or causes that unites and inspires the whole family

- Make sure that the family's charitable arm is consistent with the family's vision

- Review the family's philanthropic interests on a regular basis such as at the quarterly family meeting.

- Ensure that you get total family involvement as a philanthropic arm can help to make family members who are not directly involved in the businesses aware of and interested in the family's finances.

- Decide whether to either make direct donations or set up a family charitable trust. Make sure that the whole family agree on whichever option is taken and then obtain the best possible advice regarding the tax and legal implications once a decision has been taken.

- Consider donating assets to charities rather than just money, such as a real estate property that continually pays rent to the charity.

- Make sure that the charity is sustainable. Do your due diligence on the Trustees and the charity's financial history. Find out how much of the annual money that they raise goes to the charitable causes they allegedly support. Invest in inspiration, not desperation!

4. Aligned And Accountable Professional Advisors

Every high net worth family has a collection of *professional advisors* that help them to control and manage their finances, taxes, investments and legal requirements.

As stated, professionals can include but are not limited to:

- Lawyers
- Accountants
- Tax advisors
- Financial advisors
- Mortgage brokers
- Trustees
- Other

However, I am still amazed at how few of these advisors communicate with one another.

We have found that they are all so focused on their own goals – *to maximise fee income* – they forget to take a step back and consider what their clients actually need.

I am not placing any blame on these advisors as I am sure they are exceptionally stressed to meet their targets whilst trying their utmost to manage client expectations.

In fact, some of the blame should be placed on the clients themselves. After all, it is their responsibility to control, manage, maintain and grow the family's finances and business needs. Yet, all too often, they rely on the false premise that they and their family are protected by having an expensive team of advisors. It should be remembered that even if you are dealing with a leading partner of a top law firm, they are still answerable to their fellow partners.

We once attended a meeting with a client and his team of professional trustees who were responsible for managing a multi-million-pound portfolio of assets. We asked them a simple question, *"What would happen if the donor (the client) suddenly died?"* and the answer truly shocked us (and our client). The fact is that none of them had even bothered to ask the client what he wanted for his estate and his beneficiaries. This was yet another case of a client assuming that everything was fine.

On another occasion, we were asked to review our client's will to ensure that it was tax efficient. This will was prepared by a very large and reputable law firm, but apart from finding several spelling mistakes, we were shocked that the firm had forgotten to update the residency status of our client in the will!

Luckily, this was quickly rectified!

The fact is that all professionals are human, which means they are all capable of making mistakes.

However, none of them can be expected to understand what it is you require for you and your family. Also, they will not know if there have been any changes in your situation (such as a change of residency) unless you regularly and effectively communicate with them (see number 1 of the 4 components above).

Irrespective of the size of their firm or how much they charge, they are not mind readers! You and your family must take responsibility for your family's wealth. This may sound simple but how can you do this in practice?

Essentially, it all begins with the vision that you and the rest of your family have for your wealth. If you are unclear or do not even have a family vision, then you are planning to fail. How can your professional advisors be aligned with your family vision if you do not even have one?

Take the time to create your family vision and make sure that every family member is involved in its creation. The family must buy into the vision and believe in it, so it cannot be forced upon them. Just look at the world's most successful businesses and it is obvious that all the employees know and passionately believe in the company's vision.

The family vision should be an adaptable tool that must be reviewed and discussed at least once a year. Once it has been created, it *must* be clearly communicated with all the family's advisors so that they know any advice they provide needs to fall in line with the family's vision. It also provides a point of reference when you are keeping the advisors accountable.

Keep your professional advisors accountable

Excellent advisors love to be made accountable. Why? Quite simply, it allows them to continually show you, the client, what an amazing job they are doing and that you are getting a great return on your money (i.e., on their fees).

The only advisors who do not want to be accountable are the ones that hide behind their fees, are not acting in your best interests and are not aligned with your vision. The only issue is that dealing with professional advisors can be daunting.

Coming from a professional background, as a qualified chartered certified accountant, I recommend that you do the following before and during your meeting with your professional advisors, as it will help to empower you and ensure that the meeting is positive and productive.

Prepare an agenda for your meeting

Make sure you attend the meeting with a list of queries that you want to ask. Be clear about the outcomes that you both want and expect from your meeting and make sure every area is covered.

Ask questions

Whilst you should not interrogate your advisors, do not be afraid to ask difficult questions, such as: *'Can you please give me a breakdown of your fees and a brief explanation as to what you have charged?'*

Remember that you are the paying customer, and as such, your advisors are *always* accountable to you.

Appreciate your advisors

If they are doing a great job for and have repeatedly gone the *extra mile* for you and your family, then make sure you thank them for their service.

Your meetings provide you with a platform to not only make your advisors accountable, but also show your gratitude.

All advisors want to feel appreciated and you would be amazed at how the service will improve just by showing a little gratitude.

Never forget that your advisors are an integral part of your family's multi-generational prosperity.

Take an advisor with you

It can sometimes help to bring along another a professional advisor to your meetings.

For example, we would recommend that you take your tax advisor to meet your trustees.

Bringing along another professional advisor will help to ensure that your advisors are comfortable speaking to one another (see the next section).

More importantly, they may be able to raise questions or ideas that you have not considered such as the tax implications of undertaking certain legal advice.

Introduce family members to your advisors

One of the many weaknesses that I have found while working with families is that dealing wit advisors tends to be the responsibility of only one family member (usually the head of the family).

The reason why this is such a significant threat to your family's wealth is because all the knowledge about the family's structures and relationships with the key advisors dies with that family member.

So why take this risk? Don't leave your eggs in one basket.

It is essential that all your family members know who the key advisors are and at least two people within the family have a working relationship with them.

In addition, diversify the financial, legal and tax

responsibility among several family members. Any meeting that you have with your advisors is another opportunity for you to introduce a family member.

Encourage your advisors to work together as a team

Your advisors need to be aligned with your family's vision and their advice needs to achieve the overall objective of both sustaining and growing the family's wealth for multiple generations.

Yet advisors very rarely communicate with other advisors outside of their business, even when they are dealing with mutual clients.

In my own personal experience, I have known occasions when financial advisors did not speak with the family's tax advisors to ensure that their financial advice was tax efficient for the family and when lawyers did not communicate with the family's financial advisors to ensure that all the investments were covered in the will.

In order to guarantee the best possible advice for you and your family, it is essential that *all* your advisors communicate with each other. Although this may seem simple in theory, it can prove to be very difficult in reality. So how can you encourage your advisors to work together?

The answer is relatively straightforward – hold an annual *Board Meeting* with all your advisors at least once a year. This will ensure that you get all your advisors sitting around a table to discuss your family's needs and how they can provide the best service to you. In fact, your advisors will probably get business opportunities and even client referrals by working with each other, so it really is a win-win situation for all.

Introduce Family Members To Your Advisors

One of the many weaknesses that I have uncovered working with families is that dealing with advisors tends to be the responsibility of only one family member (usually the head of the family).

This is because all the knowledge about the family's structures and the relationships with the key advisors lies (and subsequently dies) with that family member.

Why take this risk?

It is essential that all the family members know who the key advisors are and at least two people within the family have a working relationship with them.

Don't leave your eggs in one basket and diversify financial, legal and tax responsibility amongst several family members. Any meeting that you have with your advisors is another opportunity for you to introduce a family member.

Summary Of The Four Fundamentals Of Family Prosperity

Your family deserves to retain and grow its wealth for many generations to come. Research has shown that only 30% of families will retain their wealth for two generations and less than 10% retain it for three. If you value your family and wish to utilise your wealth in a positive way, then it's essential that you start putting in place the four concepts of family prosperity today. These are:

- Effective Communication
- Wealth Education and Preparing the Heirs
- Sustainable Philanthropy
- Aligned and Accountable Professional Advisors

At this point, I want to check if this is making sense.

Have we introduced any concept that feels uncomfortable, new or challenging to you?

As I said much earlier, for some clients all of this is a learning curve because they have not appreciated the real threats and causes of multi-generational financial failure. Secretly, they feel confronted. For example, some people have been playing their cards very close to their chest for a long time so they are not sure at all about effective communication even though, in principle, it is prudent advice.

Remember, the first generation has struggled along the proverbial rags-to-riches path. Figuratively, or in actuality, they rolled up their sleeves and created the wealth, so they are highly motivated, very ambitious and even obsessive.

Often in their opinion, their children typically lack an appreciation and understanding of money and usually spend rather than accumulate wealth.

And to them, their grandchildren are even bigger spendthrifts.

Poor Traditional Professional Advice Was NOT The Issue

All these families usually have great professional advisors - accountants, lawyers, financial advisors etc. So what went wrong? The research points towards many issues but invariably the top three fundamental errors are:

- Poor communication and trust breakdown

- No clear or compelling family vision

- Failure to prepare family heirs

Yes, you need professional advice but the key mistake is everyone places too much emphasis on this.

Creating a structure that supports sustainable muti-generational family prosperity is like building a house. Like any house, the strength of the structure is based on solid foundations. *You cannot build a house by starting on the roof!* Yet families that rely solely on their professional advisors are making exactly this mistake.

To achieve family prosperity the foundation must be effective communication which is why we start right there. And so should you.

The Pyramid Of Prosperity

The four fundamentals need to be encompassed and aligned with the family's vision. When placed together they will form what we call the *Pyramid of Prosperity.*

We hope that we can be a part of your family's power team and help you and your family to integrate the four concepts into your vision. Together, we can ensure that your family's prosperity not just survives, but also thrives for many generations to come.

The Fundamental Questions You Need To Ask Regarding Your Family's Wealth Prosperity

Let's check how well you now understand the fundamentals of family prosperity. To do that we've included a short quiz. The questions below will help you to assess the risk to your family wealth. Simply answer *Yes* of *No* to the following:

1. Vision

Do you have a clear written purposeful family *vision* that moves and inspires ALL your family members?

❏ Yes ❏ No

2. Professional Advisors

Are *all* your family members familiar with who *all* your *professional advisors* are and *exactly* what they do?

❏ Yes ❏ No

3. Communication

Does your family have *highly effective communication structures* in place such as regular formal family Board meetings?

❏ Yes ❏ No

4. Family Roles

Has each family member been designated a *clear* and *formal role* within the family structure and have they bought into their roles with enthusiasm?

❏ Yes ❏ No

5. Family Structures

Does your family have a clear *wealth map* detailing the family's assets, the structures they are held in and who the advisors are for these structures?

❏ Yes ❏ No

6. Wealth Appreciation

Are you confident that your children (and grandchildren) *appreciate*, understand and value the family's wealth and investments?

❏ Yes ❏ No

7. Wealth Values

Do you know each individual family member's highest *values* and if so they aligned to wealth building?

❏ Yes ❏ No

8. Sustainable Philanthropy (Legacy)

Does your family currently have structured *sustainable philanthropy* that both inspires and is supported by each family member?

❏ Yes ❏ No

How To Score The Quiz

If you answered *No* to just one of the above questions your family wealth legacy is - statistically - at risk.

So what next?

The suggested approach is stamped *Urgent* and a confidential conversation is highly recommended.

How We Work With Clients: The Charles Group Family Prosperity Advisors

We are not financial advisors but over many years have come to recognise that if you focus on the *money first* the family falls. But if you focus on the *family first* the money follows.

Over time, we have built a highly-trusted and unique family prosperity advisory and management service for multi-millionaire families.

Over 44 years in our accountancy practice we found families with significant assets who were invariably exposed due to poor attitudes and behaviours; and poor advice or a poor family wealth strategy.

Wherever they were exposed, the family's wealth foundations were not strong enough to withstand those risks - even though they had access to good professional advice.

Our mission is to protect the family wealth for generations to come and to help you thrive.

As covered in this book we help clients establish a clear vision, a strategy, structure, processes and trusted communications that are essential for sustained family wealth.

At the *Charles Group*, we help high-net-worth families with a series of services that are focused on ensuring your family wealth will grow and not be blown in three generations.

Our clients have assets that range between three bandwidths:

• From £10 million to £25 million

• £25 million to £100 million

• Over £100 million.

Bringing It All Together

Our confidential approach includes:

- Conducting Professional Services - Connecting your family to our world class partners
- Family communication structures including formal family days
- Family vision creation
- Family Asset Protection
- Family Stewardship – preparing your heirs
- Property Mentorship
- Professional Team Building and accountability
- Family and Business Tax Planning
- Design Bespoke Sustainable Philanthropy

References

- Bonner B. and Bonner W. (2012). *Family Fortunes: How to Build Family Wealth and Hold on to it for 100 Years.* John Wiley & Sons

- Forbes Magazine – 2014 study of billionaire families Source: www.familybusinessplace.com

- George. K. (2017). *The Effective Board Member.* TGF Books

- Hughes Jr J. E. (2004). *Family Wealth – Keeping it in the Family.* Bloomberg Press

- Marcovici P. (2016). *The Destructive Power of Family Wealth.* John Wiley & Sons

- Simmons M. W. (2017). *The Rothschilds – The Dynasty and the Legacy.* Make Profits Easy LLC

- Sinek S. (2011). *Start with Why – How great leaders inspire everyone to take action.* Portfolio Penguin

- William R. & Preisser V. (2014). *Preparing Heirs.* Robert D. Reed Publishers

Acknowledgments

I would like to thank everybody who took an active role in the creation of this book. This process has helped me to truly appreciate how much of a team effort is required to put together a book.

Firstly, I would like to thank John Castagnini and his team at *Thank God I* who helped with the editing of this book. Your quality and honest feedback were always (and still are) welcomed. Initially when we started working together, you were a consultant but today I am proud to call you a partner of the *Charles Group*. Your 30 years' experience in equilibration has proven vital in helping families to deal with conflict, depression and other emotional charges which can have such a detrimental impact on family prosperity.

To Alistair Lobo, thank you for helping me to bring my vision for the *Charles Group* to life. We have been on a long but fruitful journey together and just like John you have now become a partner of the *Charles Group* helping families globally to create their vision that inspires them to create a purpose greater than themselves.

To Andrew Priestley for constantly pushing me to finish this book but more importantly helping me with everything required to get it published. Your experience as a multi-best-selling author has proven invaluable.

To all my team at *Charles Group* and *C Charles & Co* for all your hard work to keep the business moving in the right direction whilst I was writing this book. A special thank you goes out to my brother in law Dimitrios Bismpas, my cousin Demetri Demetriou and Theognosia (Soulla) Cotsapa who I have also considered my aunty. Together you are yet another example of the importance of family both in business and in life.

My grateful thanks to all my clients. Working to help you has given me world class experience on what it takes to be successful in business and invaluable insights which inspired me to create the *Four Fundamentals*. Without you this book would not have its richness and the *Charles Group* would not have existed.

I would like to thank Roy Williams and Vic Preisser for all their research over a sustained period into 3,250 families to uncover why traditional estate planning is not sufficient to help families retain and grow their wealth for multiple generations.

To my wonderful parents, Costas and Christina for doing a world class job in raising me and my siblings. Your stories are not only entertaining but inspiring. You are both my heroes and I work hard every day just to emulate your success in life. Whilst I thank you for everything you have done for me I can never fully appreciate growing up with nothing. I am forever grateful that I was born to have you as parents.

Finally, I would like to thank my wife and best friend Andrea. Her patience and support have been worldly and not always deserved. My life would be empty without her and my two amazing children. I hate to think how my life would have ended up if we never met. This book is testimony to all her hard work.

About Nicholas Charles FCCA

Nicholas Charles FCCA is a family prosperity advisor. He created the *Four Fundamentals* a bespoke programme that helps families to retain their wealth for multiple generations.

In 2009 he was recognised as a *Fellow Chartered Certified Accountant*. Nicholas specialises in family prosperity advice, tax planning, asset protection and property consultancy.

He is the CEO of the Charles Group an organisation that bridges the gap between high net worth families and their advisors. Whilst working with families to help them establish and build the *Four Fundamentals* he focuses on the one key area and the foundation for family prosperity – enhanced, effective communication both within the family and externally with their advisors.

He runs his own successful accountancy practice specialising in property tax and looks after a portfolio of high net worth property investors and developers.

Nicholas also runs a multi-million-pound property portfolio. He took over the family portfolio when it had a market value of £4m.

Today that value has quadrupled in asset value along with the rental income.

Please contact Nicholas:

Email: FamilyProsperity@CharlesGroup.co.uk

Website: www.FamilyProsperity.co.uk

Phone: (+44) 20 7263 3295